Our Leaders

by Ann-Marie Kishel

first step nonfiction

Lerner Publications Company · Minneapolis

A **leader** is the person in charge.

A good leader cares about
the people she leads.

A good leader makes our
lives better.

Some people choose to be leaders.

Parents are the leaders of
a family.

Principals and teachers are leaders at school.

We choose some leaders.

We **vote** to decide who will be in charge.

We vote for the **mayor**.

The mayor is the leader of
our city.

We vote for the **governor**.

The governor is the leader
of our state.

We vote for the **president**.

The president is the leader
of our country.

Leaders work to make our community a good place.

How can you be a leader?

What qualities does a leader have?

- A leader is honest.

- A leader is fair.

- A leader cares.

- A leader is kind.

- A leader is helpful.

How do the leaders on the next page show these qualities?

Presidential Facts

 United States citizens vote for president every four years.

 A person can be elected president only two times.

 The president is responsible for making sure people follow laws.

 The president is the head of the United States military.

 The first president of the United States was George Washington.

United Nations Facts

 The United Nations brings together leaders from many countries. The leaders work together to solve world problems. They help people have better lives.

 191 countries are members of the United Nations.

 The leader of the United Nations is called the Secretary-General. A new Secretary-General is elected every five years.

Glossary

 governor – the leader of a state

 leader – a person who is in charge

 mayor – the leader of a city or town

 president – the leader of a country

 vote – to choose

Index

The photographs in this book are reproduced through the courtesy of: © David McNew/Getty Images, cover; © PhotoDisc Royalty Free by Getty Images, pp. 2, 4; © Digital Vision by Getty Images, pp. 3, 7, 19 (top); © Tom Stewart/CORBIS, p. 5; © Stockbyte, pp. 6, 22 (second from top); © age fotostock/Superstock, p. 8; © Mike Simons/Getty Images, pp. 9, 22 (bottom); © Chris Graythen/Getty Images, pp. 10, 22 (middle); © Barry Williams/Getty Images, p. 11; © AP/Wide World Photos, pp. 12, 22 (top); Office of New Mexico Governor Bill Richardson, p. 13; © AFP/Getty Images, p. 14; © Chip Somodevilla/Getty Images, pp. 15, 22 (second from bottom); © Jim West/Zuma Press, p. 16; © Todd Strand/Independent Picture Service, p. 17; © Mario Tama/Getty Images, p. 19 (middle); © Brand X Pictures, p. 19 (bottom).

Lerner Publishing Company
A division of Lerner Publishing Group
241 First Avenue North
Minneapolis, MN 55401 U.S.A.

Website address: www.lernerbooks.com

Library of Congress Cataloging-in-Publication Data

Kishel, Ann-Marie.
    Our leaders / by Ann-Marie Kishel.
        p.   cm. — (First step nonfiction)
    Includes index.
    ISBN-13: 978–0–8225–6395–2 (lib. bdg. : alk. paper)
    ISBN-10: 0–8225–6395–9 (lib. bdg. : alk. paper)
    1. Leadership—Juvenile literature. 2. Political leadership—United States—Juvenile literature. I. Title.
    HM1261.K5 2007
    303.3'40973—dc22   2006018516

Manufactured in the United States of America
1 2 3 4 5 6 – DP – 12 11 10 09 08 07